Roister Doister Publishing

Housebound

by Simon Mawdsley

WWW.ROSITERDOISTER.COM

About the Author
Simon Mawdsley

Housebound was first performed at Victoria Hall Theatre, Old Harlow September 2012.

CAST

Bone   Martin Bedwell

Fiona   Caroline Petherbridge

PRODUCTION TEAM

Director   Simon Mawdsley

Designer   Jonathan Chinsky

Housebound

A One Act Play

by Simon Mawdsley

HOUSEBOUND

Morning.

A tastefully furnished living room in a detached house in suburbia. A door to the kitchen stage left, and a door to the hall stage right. A sofa, upstage, a cabinet or sideboard stage left with a house phone, an I-pod player and a box of tissues on it. There is a small table by the window, stage right, with a bowl of pot pouri on it. A small waste-paper bin and a magazine rack on the floor.

Classical music (suggestion: Vaughan Williams The Wasps) is playing, loudly.

As the lights come up we find Fiona, late 30's, wearing a dressing gown, tied to a dining chair, blind-folded, her mouth taped. Behind her stands Bone, late '50's, wearing a donkey jacket, gloves, a face-mask, holding a handgun. He checks that Fiona is securely tied and the blind-fold is secure, then checks the room, the doors, the windows. He looks round for the source of the music – the I-pod player. He doesn't know how to work it so pulls the mains cord out. He removes the mask. He puts the gun down carefully on the sideboard, removes one glove with his teeth, takes out a handkerchief and wipes the sweat from his face. He takes out a mobile phone, dials a number.

Bone
(Into phone) **Sorted.**

He puts the phone away, then checks on Fiona again. She is sitting bolt upright. The reality of the situation seems to hit him now, and for a moment he considers giving up and getting out, but takes a breath and crosses to Fiona

Bone
Look, I'm not gonna hurt you - nothin' bad is gonna happen - just as long as you do exactly what I tell you. Okay? Okay? Now, listen; I'm gonna take the tape off your mouth, okay? But you gotta promise me you won't start screamin'. No-one's gonna hear you if you do and all that's gonna happen is I'm gonna put the tape straight back on again' okay? Just nod your head if you understand.

She nods, and he carefully removes the tape and stands back. She hyperventilates for a few moments, before her breathing begins to even out.

Bone
Right, just try and... Just don't worry. I know this is tough, but... Fiona: Sick.

Bone
What?

Fiona
Feel sick.

Bone
Shit.

He looks around the room, finds a waste-paper bin, and holds it under her chin. She retches and retches, but nothing much comes out.

Bone
Done?

She nods. He puts down the waste-paper bin, takes a tissue from the box, and gently wipes the corner of her mouth.

Fiona
Thank you.

Bone
You alright? Sorry, stupid question. I'm…

Fiona
(She takes a breath) Jewellery upstairs – bedroom – in a box - Chinese – on the dressing table. That's all. No money in the house - just in my purse –

Bone
Yeah, look -

Fiona
In the kitchen - in my handbag.

Bone
I'm not –

Fiona
There's no hidden safe, I promise you, nothing like that. Please – please don't tear the house up –

Bone
I won't, I –

Fiona
We've just had the carpets laid -

Bone
Right.

Fiona
It's Merino Wool.

Bone
Oh.

Fiona
Royal Wilton.

Bone
Nice.

Fiona
Could you take your shoes off?

Bone
What?

Fiona
If you go upstairs – only, it rained last night, and you came in from the garden, and it's quite muddy and I don't...

Bone
I'm not goin' upstairs! I don't want your jewellery, and I don't want your carpet.

Fiona
Oh.

Bone
I'm not here for that. This isn't a burglary.

Fiona
Oh. *(A moment of realisation.)* Oh God! Oh no! No, no, no, no –

Bone
What? Oh shit! No, no, no, no – *(They're both shouting "no".)* - look, it's not that either. Nothing like that! Calm down.

He puts his hand on her shoulder – she screams! He leaps back - checks the window to see if anyone heard her.

Bone
Listen! – listen to me – I'm not gonna touch you. Okay? I – am - not - goin' - to touch you.

She very gradually pulls herself together.

Fiona
What? What is it that you want?

Bone
Right. In about five minutes your husband –

Fiona
My husband!?

Bone
- is gonna be...

Fiona
What, Keith?

Bone
Keith. Your husband. Yes.

Fiona
What's he done?

Bone
Nothing. Listen. In about five minutes he'll be arrivin' at work...

Fiona
At the bank?

Bone
At the bank. And when he does my associate will call me, and then you will call him and explain that...

Fiona
Call your associate?

Bone
No, your husband. You call him and tell him that I am here and...

Fiona
Oh, I see – I'm a hostage.

Bone
You tell him I'm here, with a gun, and you give him instructions.

Fiona
What instructions?

Bone
I've got 'em written down – you just read 'em out.

Fiona
To Keith?

Bone
Your husband.

Fiona
What about the blindfold? I can't read if I'm wearing a...

Bone
When the time comes I'll take it off.

Fiona
Can't you take it off now?

Bone
No.

Fiona
Why not?

Bone
Because I don't want you to see my face.

Fiona
But you're wearing a mask.

Bone
I took it off.

Fiona
Can't you put it back on again?

Bone
No. I can't. I don't want to. It's hot and it makes my face itch.

Fiona
But you couldn't you just…?

Bone
No – I couldn't! Just shut up and listen!

She starts crying, hyperventilating…

Bone
Sorry. But you just need to listen – this is important. *(Sees she's struggling.)* Look, just… breathe, okay? Breathe! Easy, easy. That's it - in and out. In… and out. In…

Fiona
Please don't shout.

Bone
Okay.

Fiona
I suffer from anxiety. Quite badly. I get panic attacks. I really don't want to go to pieces. If I lose control of myself then I won't be able to…

Bone
Fair enough.

Fiona
When you shout it just makes me…

Bone
Point taken.

Fiona
And…

Bone
What?

Fiona
Would you mind… not moving about so much. Not being able to see anything – it's disorientating – not knowing where you are.

Bone
(Under his breath.) Fuckin' 'ell.

Fiona
Pardon?

Bone
I'll try not to move about so much.

Fiona
You want me to be calm. I'm trying to be. I'm really trying.

Bone
You really are.

Fiona
You see, if you could just take the blindfold off, I…

Bone
No way.

Fiona
For just a moment.

Bone
No.

A moment.
Fiona
You want the instructions to be clear, don't you?

Bone
Yeah.

Fiona
But if I start to panic I might not be able to read them. I might get it all wrong. I'm not very good under pressure. I might get sick again. If… if I could read through them beforehand – rehearse them. Just for a minute. It would help. You needn't put the mask back on – you could just stand behind me. I wouldn't look.

No answer.

Hello?

No answer.

What are you doing?

Bone
Thinkin'.

Fiona
Okay.

A moment. He thinks.

Bone
You promise not to look?

Fiona
Cross my heart.

Standing behind her, he takes off the blind-fold.

Bone
One minute. Okay?

Fiona
Yes. Thank you. Thank you. (blinking) It's very bright. Could you draw the curtains?

Bone
No. Here.

He hands her a folded scrap of paper.

Fiona
You're going to have to hold it for me.

Bone
What? Oh.

He unfolds the piece of paper and holds it in front of her.

Fiona
Too close.

Bone
(Holding it further away.) Better?

Fiona
(Squinting) Bit more. That's… No, too far – back a bit. Right, just there please.

Bone
Okay?

Fiona
So this is what you want me to say to Keith?

Bone
Just read it. Hurry up.

Fiona
(Clears her throat, and reads haltingly.) "Hello... this is... your... life"

Bone
Wife. This is your wife.

Fiona
Of course. This is your wife. The hand-writing's terrible.

Bone
Get on with it.

Fiona
"Hello, this is your wife..." Actually, I wouldn't say that.

Bone
What?

Fiona
I wouldn't say "This is your wife." I'd never say that. I'd say; "this is Fiona"

Bone
Say that then, it don't matter. Come on.

Fiona
Sorry, could you keep it still please? I can't focus. Thank you. Okay, so "Hello Keith, this is Fiona. Listen.. carefully..." What if he doesn't?

Bone
Doesn't what?

Fiona
Listen carefully. He hates me calling him at work, he's always too busy. I mean, he doesn't listen to me at the best of times, let alone...

Bone
He'll listen.

Fiona
That's if I can get through. You have to get past his secretary first. Melinda. She's quite, well, snotty. She fields his calls. Even from me.

Bone
You tell her it's urgent. Read!

Fiona
Sorry. "Listen carefully there. Is a...?" - Oh, I see, "listen carefully – comma – there is a... nun?"

Bone
Man.

Fiona
"Man.. with a… grin…"

Bone
Gun!

Fiona
Gun – yes, of course. "… man with a gun to my… beard?"

Bone
(Snatching the paper away.) Are you takin' the piss?

Fiona
No, really, I'm not.

Bone
Gun to my head! My head!

Fiona
It looks like beard.

Bone
Why would it be beard?!

Fiona
You're shouting.

Bone
That's right – I am! I knew this was a bad idea.

Fiona
I'm sorry. Let me try again. Please.

He places the instructions in front of her again…

Bone
Go.

Fiona
"…Man holding a gun to my head. So you got to do… exactly what I tell you. Don't do… nothing stupid." Um…?

Bone
Now what?

Fiona
Would you mind if I paraphrase?

Bone
Do what?

Fiona
Paraphrase. Put it another way. It's just that – no offence – but the grammar is a bit….

Bone
What?

Fiona
Did you write this?

Bone
Yes. Get on with it.

Fiona
"In a… snort.. In a short while a man… will…" - I'm sorry, it's no good.

Bone
What now?

Fiona
It's just a blur. I need my glasses. My reading glasses.

Bone
Fucksake.

Fiona
They're in the kitchen.

Bone
I don't believe this.

Fiona
On the work-top. By the terracotta storage jars, I think.

Bone turns to go, then turns back and puts the blindfold back on Fiona.

Fiona
I wasn't going to look. Really.

Bone exits to the kitchen. Fiona struggles with her bonds. After a few moments we hear Bone cry out from the kitchen.

Bone
(Off) SHIT!

(He stumbles backwards into the room.)

Oh shit, shit!

Fiona
What?!

Bone
Wasp!

Fiona
What!?

Bone
WASP!

Fiona
Where!?

Bone
In the kitchen! Dirty great –

Fiona
Oh God!

Bone
– Fucker! Flew right at me!

Fiona
Oh no!

Bone
Size of it! Bastard!

Fiona
Is it –?

Bone
Right at me!

Fiona
Did it –?

Bone
What?

Fiona
Follow you?

Bone
Follow me?

Fiona
Is it in here!?

Bone
No.

Fiona
Are you sure!

Bone
YES, I'M SURE!!

Fiona
DON'T SHOUT!

Bone
SORRY!!

They both take time to pull themselves together, both breathing in and out, almost in unison.

Bone
You alright?

Fiona
I hate wasps.

Bone
Me too. Always have. Can't be in the same room with one.

Fiona
At least you could run.

Bone
What?

Fiona
What do you think it's like to be tied up and blind-folded with a wasp loose in the room?

Bone
Yeah, but it wasn't in the room, was it?

Fiona
I wasn't to know that, was I? You suddenly start screaming "wasp!"

Bone
I wasn't screaming.

Fiona
It can't get in, can it?

Bone
Not unless it can open doors. Mind you, it was big enough. Enormous.

Fiona
It could have been a hornet.

Bone
Or a queen.

Fiona
Oh God. If it's a queen it might nest. There might be a swarm.

Bone
There weren't no swarm.

Fiona
Can you check?

Bone
I ain't goin' back in there.

Fiona
You've got a gun.

A moment, then Bone laughs.

What?
Bone
Not much of a tough guy, am I?

Fiona
Do you think you could take the blind-fold off? Please? I know the wasp isn't in here, but it would help if I could see for myself.

Bone
You know, my Mum used to say that if you close your eyes, stand perfectly still and count to ten, they just go away.

Fiona
Did it work?

Bone
Dunno. Never managed to get past three. *(He takes the blindfold off.)* I'm trusting you not to look round.

Fiona
I won't.

Bone
Fix your eyes straight ahead.

Fiona
I will. What about my arms?

Bone
No.

Fiona
They're really beginning to ache.

Bone
I said no.

A moment.

Fiona
There's no need to feel embarrassed.

Bone
About what?

Fiona
The w-a-s-p.

Bone
(Spells it in his head.) I'm not.

Fiona
Even the bravest people have phobias.

Bone
It ain't a phobia. They just scare the shit outa me.

Fiona
Me too. What about bees?

Bone
Bees are okay.

Fiona
Spiders?

Bone
It's just wasps I hate.

Fiona
You're lucky. I have a problem with most insects – ones that crawl, ones that fly…

Bone
(Not really listening.) Yeah?

Fiona
And mice. And frogs. And birds – when they get inside buildings. I'm okay with them outside, as long as they don't get too near.

Bone
Right.

Fiona
Dogs. Crowds. Bridges. Deep water. Umbrellas.

Bone
Umbrellas?

Fiona
Just black ones.

Bone
Jesus. You don't get out much then?

Fiona
I'm agoraphobic.

Bone
I don't blame you.

Fiona
No, it means…

Bone
I know what it means. Fear of open spaces.

Fiona
No, that's what everyone thinks. It's actually a fear of what might happen to you in a public place, of not being able escape, of just going to pieces.

Bone
So you don't go out at all?

Fiona
There are phases when it isn't as severe. I might be able to get to the shops. But recently I haven't been out at all.

Bone
I know.

A beat.

Fiona
You know?

Bone
Eh?

Fiona
How do you know? You've been watching the house, haven't you?

Bone
I… erm…

Fiona
You must have been, to know I'd be here. Oh, that's horrible. Knowing that you've been out there, watching me -

Bone
Not watching you, just the 'ouse.

Fiona
- Looking through the windows.

Bone
No. Look, I'm not a peeping Tom.

Fiona
I've gone all cold.

Bone
It's nothing personal.

Fiona
Yes it is. It couldn't be more personal.

Bone
Sorry love, just the way it is.

Fiona
Fiona.

Bone
Eh?

Fiona
My name is Fiona.

Bone
(Flatly) Nice to meet you. *(To the 'phone.)* Come on, come on, come on.

A moment.

Fiona
You're not going to hurt him, are you?

Bone
Who?

Fiona
Keith.

Bone
No.

Fiona
You promise?

Bone
Look, all that happens is you give him the instructions, he hands over the money, and we walk away. Simple. Job done.

Fiona
The instructions - did you get my reading glasses?

Bone
What? Oh bollocks!

Fiona
You could just read them out to me. I could memorise them.

Bone
Yeah? *(She nods.)* Okay, hold on. *(Takes out the instructions and reads.)* "blah, blah, blah, man with a gun to my…" – that looks nothing like beard. "So you got to do exactly what…"

Fiona
I know that bit. Skip forward.

Bone
Right, so; "At nine o'clock this morning a man will come into the bank and ask to see you. He will make himself known as Mister Brown…"

Fiona
Mister Brown?

Bone
Mister Brown.

Fiona
Couldn't you think of a more original name?

Bone
No. "You will take him to your office…"

Fiona
What if a real Mister Brown turns up at the same time? It's a very common name, and…

Bone
(Raising his voice.) "You will take him to your office and give him one hundred thousand pounds in cash."

Fiona
He won't do it, you know.

Bone
What?

Fiona
He won't give you the money.

Bone
He'll do it.

Fiona
I'm telling you he won't. He's too stubborn.

Bone
He's not gonna risk any…

Fiona
Anything happening to me? You don't know him. He'll call your bluff.

Bone
He better not.

Fiona
Or what?

Bone
It won't come to that.

Fiona
What if it does?

Bone
It won't.

Fiona
I'm telling you it will. Then what? Are you going to shoot me?

Bone
No.

Fiona
Torture me?

Bone
(Angry) I'll tell you what I'll do if you don't shut up – I'm gonna tape your mouth back up. And put the blind-fold on. And then.. then I'm gonna go out and get my boots all muddy, and trample them all over your nice, new carpet, alright?!

Fiona hangs her head. Bone paces. His mobile rings.

Bone
(On 'phone.) Yeah? – What? – Where the…? – You sure you 'aven't missed him? – How the hell should I know?! – No, I saw him drive off. – Oh, this is…

Fiona
Dentist!

Bone
Hold on. *(Turns to her.)* What you say?

Fiona
Keith – he's at the dentist. I just remembered. He had an early morning appointment.

Bone
Why the hell didn't you…?

Fiona
Sorry. I forgot.

Bone
I don't fuckin' believe this! *(Back on 'phone.)* Apparently he's at the dentist. – I dunno – *(To Fiona.)* What for?

18

Fiona
Pardon?

Bone
What's he at the dentist for?

Fiona
Wisdom tooth.

Bone
(Phone) Wisdom tooth. *(To Fiona)* Check-up or treatment?

Fiona
Check-up.

Bone
(Phone) Check up.

Fiona
They've been giving him gyp for ages, and I kept saying he should go, but he really doesn't like…

Bone "shushes" her.

Bone
(Phone) No way. – That's easy for you to say, I'm the one who… - I don't care, it's… *(Turning away from Fiona.)* Look, I can't stay cooped up in here, it's doin' my head in. – No, she's just… - I know that, but… - Alright. But that's it. Not a minute longer. – Yeah. *(Hangs up.)* Bollocks. Bollocks! *(Takes off his jacket and throws it on the floor.)*

Fiona
What was that?

Bone
My jacket. I just threw it on the floor.

Fiona
There's a peg in the hall if you want to hang it up.

Bone
No, I don't want to fuckin' 'ang it up!

A moment.

Fiona
There's no need to swear. I know you're angry – and it's my fault for not remembering his appointment - but when you shout and swear like that, it scares me.

Bone
I'm not angry with you.

Fiona
Really?

Bone
Really.

Fiona
So, what happens now?

Bone
We give him half-an-hour. If he don't show up by then, I'm off.

Bone sits down on the sofa.

Fiona
I should have said he was having treatment, shouldn't I? If I'd have said he was having his teeth out you wouldn't have waited. Oh, I'm so stupid. Talk first, think later – that's always been my problem.

Bone
Urrggh!, What the f...

Fiona
What's wrong?

Bone
(Standing up.) I just sat in something.

Fiona
Weetabix.

Bone
What?

Fiona
It's probably Weetabix. I wondered where it ended up.

Bone
That's disgusting.

Fiona
I'm so sorry. We had a bit of a row – Keith lost his temper and threw his cereal bowl across the room.

Bone
What he do that for?

Fiona
I put too much milk on it. He doesn't like it soggy.

Bone
It's all up me trousers.

Fiona
He shouted at me, and I said he should make his own bloody breakfast, and things escalated and he ended up hurling the bowl across the room. Then he stormed out.

Bone
Yeah, he looked a bit pissed off when he left. Reversed on to the street like a lunatic.

Fiona
He was stressed about going to the dentist – I shouldn't have snapped at him.

Bone
No, you shoulda thrown the bowl right back at him.

Fiona
Oh no. I couldn't do that. Look there's a cloth in the kitchen if you want to… Oh no, you can't, can you?

Bone
It's alright.

A moment.

Fiona
Am I really doing your head in?

Bone
What?

Fiona
That's what you said to your friend just now.

Bone
You shouldn'ta been listenin'.

Fiona
That's what Keith says – that I'm doing his head in. Not the sort of phrase you'd expect from a bank manager is it? But it comes out when he's angry – his background. He can sound quite common. Sorry – no offence.

Bone
None taken.

Fiona
I don't mean to "do his head in". I probably just talk too much I suppose *(Bone nods his head behind her.)* But that's all I want to do, when he comes home from work – talk to him. Trouble is I haven't really got anything interesting to say, because I haven't been anywhere, or done anything. And the last thing he wants to do after a stressful day at work is listen to me droning on about nothing.

Bone
Well, you'll have something interestin' to talk about tonight, won't you?
Fiona: Yes. That's true. Well, thank you for that.

Bone
Welcome.

He starts pacing again.

Fiona
You'll wear the carpet out if you're not careful.

Bone
Sorry.

Fiona
It's alright. I do it all the time. It's the only exercise I get. Talk to myself, too. It's a wonder I don't do my own head in.

Bone
First sign of madness.

Fiona
Don't say that.

Bone
Joke.

Fiona
I know, but I…. I worry. Worry that I might… You know.

Bone
It ain't easy.

Fiona
Being cooped up?

Bone
No.

Fiona
Sometimes I feel as though….

Bone
Like you're in a bubble.

Fiona
Yes.

Bone
And you wonder if the outside world's still there?

Fiona
Yes! Yes, that's exactly it.

Bone
Too much time on your hands. That's what it does.

Fiona
I suppose so. It's odd, but when I had a job I used to wish there were more hours in the day – time to do all the things I promised myself I'd do. Now I have that time – so much of it – and I don't really do anything. It's criminal.

Bone
You should find a hobby.

Fiona
I know, I know. Gardening - I'd really like to do gardening. Only…

Bone
Wasps.

Fiona
And other creepy-crawlies.

Bone
Bit of a drawback.

Fiona
Or learn to play the piano.

Bone
Have you got a piano?

Fiona
No. I love music. Sometimes it's the only thing that gets me through the day.

Bone
What was that you were playin' when I come in?

Fiona
Vaughan Williams. Did you like it?

Bone
Wasn't really listenin', to be honest.

Fiona
Oh you should. He's very good.

Bone
Not really into classical music. More of a reggae man.

Fiona
Reggae? I've never really… It all sounds the same to me.

Bone
No, no, no – I used to think that. But I had this mate – Jamaican guy - who sort of educated me. There's so much more to it than the stuff you hear on the radio.

Fiona
Really?

Bone
Oh yeah. Ska – Dub – Roots – Lovers Rock…

Fiona
Lovers Rock?

Bone
My favourite style of reggae. Sweet sound. *(In a Jamaican accent.)* "If you listen," my Jamaican friend would say, "If you listen careful, you can hear the sunshine" And it's true. Sunshine in every note.

A moment of reverie.

Fiona
We went to Barbados once. Many years ago.

Bone
What was it like?

Fiona
Don't know - I spent most of it in the hotel room. May as well have stayed at home.

Bone
My mate was from Kingston.

Fiona
Upon-Thames?

Bone
Jamaica. He used to tell me all about it.

Fiona
You were in prison together?

Bone
Yeah, we… How d'you know that ?

Fiona
I guessed. All that stuff about being cooped up.

Bone
Right. You ain't the only one who talks too much.

Fiona
Were you in there a long time?

Bone
Too long and too often.

Fiona
What was it like?

Bone
Much like this – but without the pot pouri. No offence.

Fiona
None taken. I feel like I'm in prison sometimes. Only I haven't done anything wrong. Seems so unfair. I look out the window and see people walking by, and I think; why are you out there and I'm in here? Why do I have to be like this? Why do I have to be me?

Bone
Yeah, I know that feeling.

Fiona
At least you had a choice.

Bone
Did I?

Fiona
You didn't have to do whatever it was you did.

Bone
Maybe not.

Fiona
And you don't have to do this. You can walk away, right now.

Bone
I can't do that. I'm sorry.

Fiona
I can tell your heart isn't in it. Why risk going back to prison?

Bone
Ain't as simple as that.

Fiona
Why not? What are you afraid of?

Bone
(*Irritated.*) Nothin'. I ain't afraid of nothin', alright?

Fiona
Anything.

Bone
What?

Fiona
Not afraid of anything.

Bone
Right.

Fiona
Except wasps.

Bone
Except wasps.

A moment.

Fiona
If it wasn't for the one in the kitchen we could have a cup of tea.

Bone
Eh?

Fiona
A cup of tea – while we're waiting. If it wasn't for the wasp.

Bone
I s'pose.

Fiona
A cup of tea and a cigarette.

Bone
D'you smoke then?

Fiona
Sometimes.

Bone
Have you got any?

Fiona
Yes.

Bone
Here?

Fiona
Yes.

Bone
Where?

Fiona
In the kitchen.

Bone
Bugger.

Fiona
Sorry.

Bone goes to the door to the kitchen.

Bone
Whereabouts?

Fiona
In the washing machine.

Bone
What?

Fiona
In the washing machine. Keith doesn't know I smoke – he hates it. So I keep them hidden.

Bone
In the washing machine?

Fiona
It's the one place he never goes. Ridiculous isn't it?

Bone
I keep mine in the shed. My Missus don't approve neither.

Fiona
You have a wife?

Bone
Yeah, and a shed.

Fiona
Sorry, I didn't mean to sound so surprised.

Bone
She hates me smokin'. She hates just about everything I do. Spent years livin' without me – got her own routine. Then I move back home and disrupt it all. Get under her feet, leave the bog seat up, snore, watch the wrong things on telly.

Fiona
Yes – I do that too, apparently.

Bone
Kids are all grown up – they hardly know me. I think I embarrass them. So I spend most o' the time in the shed – out of the way. Out of the way of the world.

Fiona
Is that why you're doing this? Are you...?

Bone
No more questions, okay? Enough. *(Picks up a magazine, rolls it up.)* Washing machine?

Fiona
Yes.

Bone
Right, I'm goin' in.

Fiona
Good luck.

Bone takes a deep breath and exits into the kitchen. Fiona instantly begins wriggling her wrists, and quickly gets them free. She gets up and runs to the other door (s/r) but can't bring herself to go out. She turns and picks up the gun, just as Bone enters with the newspaper and the cigarettes.

Bone
I got 'em. No matches though... *(Sees her)* Oh shit.

Fiona
(Her voice high, but determined.) Don't move!

Bone
I'm not.

Fiona
Right! Right! Sit down.

Bone
You said don't move.

Fiona
Look, just do it.

Bone
Don't be silly Fiona, put it down.

Fiona
Don't tell me what to do! And don't call me silly! I am not silly!

Bone
Alright, calm down.

Fiona
I AM CALM!

Bone
Okay.

Fiona
I am calm and I am in control *(She breathes deep and evenly.)* Now sit down.

Bone
(Sits on the chair.) What you gonna do?

Fiona
I'm going to call the police.

Bone
That might be tricky. You'd have to dial with one hand and hold the gun with the other. Take your eyes off me for a second and I'll…

Fiona
Don't you try anything!

Bone
Or what? You gonna shoot me Fiona?

Fiona
I might. I'm angry enough. I am so angry with you.

Bone
Fair enough.

Fiona
You force your way into my home and tie me up and shout and swear at me and scare me to death.

Bone
Look…

Fiona
Don't say "look" I hate it when people say "look". It's always so bloody patronising and condescending. Keith always says "look".

Bone
Sorry. I am. Really sorry about all of this.

Fiona
Sorry now. Now that I'm holding the gun.

Bone
I was sorry as soon as I stepped through the door.

Fiona
Then why didn't you stop?

Bone
I dunno. Once you get caught up in these things – once you get talked into doin' something – it's hard to back out. I ain't a violent man – this ain't my sort of thing at all.

Fiona
Why were you in prison then?

Bone
Burglary. That's all.

Fiona
Oh, and I suppose that's okay is it? Breaking into people's houses and stealing their property. It's still a violation.

Bone
I never broke in while people were there. And I never left a mess. One time I broke into this house, they'd left the iron on. I turned it off – house would have burnt down otherwise.

Fiona
Oh, aren't you the good Samaritan?

Bone
No. I'm not.

Fiona
You should be ashamed of yourself.

Bone
I am.

Fiona
How would you like it if someone did this to your wife.

Bone
I wouldn't.

Fiona
So why do it to me?

Bone
Because I'm a stupid bastard. And I was desperate. I got nothin' – no money, no future, no family anymore, not really. Then someone says they got this job set-up – fool-proof, quick, piss-easy. And I think, maybe if I had that much money I could get away, right away, start a new life – in Jamaica maybe. And I think, if I don't do this job someone else will. Someone who I ain't as considerate as me. Think about that, eh? You coulda had some ravin' psycho in here instead of me?

Fiona
Am I supposed to be grateful?

Bone
No, but I didn't hurt you, did I?

Fiona
You did actually. You gave me a Chinese burn when you tied me up.

Bone
Sorry. I never intended to hurt you.

Fiona
(Waving the gun at him.) What's this for then?

Bone
It's not loaded.

Fiona
What!?

Bone
The gun's not loaded. It was just for show.

Fiona's phone rings. They both stare at it. A second later Bone's mobile rings. They look at each other. Fiona answers hers first. Then Bone answers his.

Fiona
-Hello?

Bone
- Yeah?

Fiona
- Keith.

Bone
- What is it?

Fiona
- Are you alright?

Bone
- No, nothin'.

Fiona
- Good. That's good.

Bone
- No it's not.

Fiona
- Nothing's wrong.

Bone
- It's the radio.

Fiona
- It's the television.

Bone
- No, hold on a minute.

He covers the phone and listens to Fiona.

Fiona
- Your diary? – No, I haven't. – In the kitchen? No I can't. – Because there's a wasp in there. – Yes, a wasp, W-A-S-P. – No, I won't. – Yes, Keith, it is pathetic. – Yes, I am silly. – No, you "look". – Good-bye. Have a good day at the bank.

She hangs up. She looks at Bone. He looks at her, then...

Bone
(Into 'phone.) It's over. – No, I'm done. *(Hangs up.)*

A moment.

Fiona
You're a lot older. than I thought you'd be.

Bone
Am I?

Fiona
And shorter.

Bone
I do try to be taller.

Fiona
Not what I imagined at all.

Bone
What did you imagine?

Fiona
Someone less ordinary I suppose.

Bone
Sorry to disappoint.

Fiona
What are you going to do?

Bone
You're the one in charge.

Fiona
Am I?

Bone
If you call the police they're gonna put me away. For the rest of my sorry life. Probably what I deserve, but I don't think I could face that.

Fiona
Being cooped up?

Bone
Down to you. I won't force you.

Fiona considers for a moment, then hands him the gun.

Fiona
You'd better have this.

Bone
I'll get rid of it. Hate guns. Never even held one before.

Fiona
Me neither.

Bone
You did alright.

Fiona
Thank you.

Bone
Very brave.

Fiona
Not brave enough to run out the door when I had the chance.

Bone
(Hands her the cigarettes.) Here. You probably need one.

Fiona
Thank you.

Bone
Right.

Fiona
You'd better go.

Bone
Yeah.

Fiona
Could leave the back way please?

Bone
Sure.

Fiona
I don't want the neighbours to.. You know.

Bone
No, that's fine.

Fiona
Be careful when you climb over the wall – there's some begonias that are just starting to come through.

Bone
Yeah – I saw them on the way in. Very nice. I'll be careful.

Fiona
Don't let the wasp in, will you?

Bone
No. I'll try not to. Remember what my Mum said, eh?

Fiona
Close your eyes, stand perfectly still and count to ten.

Bone
And they just disappear.

Fiona
(Closes her eyes.) One – two – three….

As she counts Bone slips away.

Slow fade to black as "Kingston Town" by Lord Creator plays out.

The End

Roister Doister Publishing

Founded in 2013 Roister Doister Publishing was created to rethink theatrical publishing, give a quality start to new writers and a more 'in touch' approach to established writers. Roister Doister Publishing endeavours to make writing, publishing, and producing theatre as easy as possible for both professionals and amateurs.

HOW DOES ROISTER DOISTER PUBLISHING DIFFER FROM OTHER PUBLISHERS?

Upfront and Up-to-date Information

All the information you need to make a decision regarding a play will be at your disposal from the moment you look at our website. License fees, availability, and permissions will all be on the play's Roister Doister page enabling you to make the right decision for your company.

Quality Control

Unlike other online 'publishers' we will not just blindly accept any script for 'publication'. We will give each script submitted to us careful consideration and advice before we release it to the public, even in our New Work section.

Investment in our Playwrights

All great theatre begins with a great play. We will invest in our writer's work and creative property by not only providing a store front for their scripts but also a professional profile for the writer where they can build their public awareness.

IF YOU ENJOYED THIS SCRIPT PLEASE ASK YOUR LOCAL
LIBRARY TO STOCK OUR TITLES

www.ingramcontent.com/pod-product-compliance
Lightning Source LLC
Chambersburg PA
CBHW061307040426
42444CB00010B/2556